PRINCEWILL LAGANG

60. "Desert Mirage: Unraveling the Wealth of Qatar

First published by PRINCEWILL LAGANG 2023

Copyright © 2023 by Princewill Lagang

All rights reserved. No part of this publication may be reproduced, stored or transmitted in any form or by any means, electronic, mechanical, photocopying, recording, scanning, or otherwise without written permission from the publisher. It is illegal to copy this book, post it to a website, or distribute it by any other means without permission.

Princewill Lagang asserts the moral right to be identified as the author of this work.

First edition

This book was professionally typeset on Reedsy.
Find out more at reedsy.com

Contents

1	Desert Mirage - Unraveling the Wealth of Qatar	1
2	Sands of Time	4
3	Pearls of Heritage	7
4	Echoes of the Past	10
5	The Modern Oasis	13
6	Beyond the Horizon	16
7	The Tapestry Unraveled	19
8	The Ongoing Odyssey	22
9	Quest for Unity	25
10	A Future Unwritten	28
11	Building the Dream	31
12	The Ever-Evolving Legacy	34
13	Summary	37

1

Desert Mirage - Unraveling the Wealth of Qatar

The sun hung low on the horizon, casting a fiery glow across the vast expanse of the Qatari desert. The shifting sands stretched out seemingly endless, a mesmerizing tapestry of dunes and silence, broken only by the occasional whisper of the desert wind. Here, where the desert met the sea, lay the small yet affluent nation of Qatar, a land of paradoxes, of ancient traditions and modern opulence.

Amidst the desolation of the arid landscape, an architectural marvel rose in stark contrast. The skyline of Doha, the capital of Qatar, glittered with a shimmering array of glass and steel towers that seemed to sprout from the sand itself. In this city of extremes, where tradition intertwined with opulence, an unparalleled wealth was cloaked in a mirage of progress and power. This paradox, this mirage, is what we shall begin to unravel.

Dr. Sarah Reynolds, a British archaeologist and professor, stood at the edge of the dunes, gazing out at the cityscape that was so incongruent with the archeological mysteries she had spent her career studying. Her fascination with Qatar had begun long before she received an invitation to speak at the prestigious Qatar National Museum. The desert, a realm that concealed countless secrets beneath its shifting sands, had always drawn her in.

As a scholar of ancient civilizations and a seeker of historical truths, Sarah was irresistibly drawn to the juxtaposition of tradition and modernity in Qatar. The nation's wealth, derived primarily from its vast reserves of oil and natural gas, had transformed it from a modest fishing and pearl-diving community to one of the richest countries in the world within a few short decades. The rapid development of Doha was a testament to this transformation.

Sarah couldn't help but feel a sense of urgency as she looked at the rapidly changing landscape. The desert's secrets were slowly fading away beneath the weight of progress, and she was determined to uncover and preserve the history that was at risk of being forgotten.

But as Sarah embarked on her quest to unearth Qatar's historical treasures, she soon discovered that the desert was not the only place where secrets lay hidden. The labyrinthine corridors of power, the intricacies of geopolitics, and the dynamic interplay of cultural traditions and modern ambitions were equally mysterious. In her pursuit of knowledge, she would find herself navigating a complex web of wealth, politics, and the enduring spirit of the Qatari people.

In this journey of exploration and discovery, Sarah Reynolds would come to understand that Qatar was much more than a land of lavish extravagance and towering skyscrapers; it was a nation rich in heritage, aspirations, and the delicate balance between preserving the past and forging a future. Desert Mirage was a story not just of Qatar's wealth but of its soul, waiting to be unveiled, one layer at a time.

With her heart full of curiosity and her mind teeming with questions, Sarah took her first step into the sands of Qatar, ready to embark on a remarkable expedition into the heart of this desert mirage, determined to reveal its hidden treasures and unlock the secrets that lay beneath the glimmering facade of opulence.

And so, the journey began, a quest to understand the essence of Qatar - a land where ancient history met the future, where a desert mirage concealed more than met the eye, and where the world's attention was drawn by an irresistible force that seemed to defy the sands of time.

2

Sands of Time

The Qatari desert had always held a mysterious allure for Dr. Sarah Reynolds. Its vast, shifting sands concealed the remnants of ancient civilizations, and it was this rich archaeological tapestry that had drawn her to Qatar. As she embarked on her quest to unravel the country's wealth and history, she knew that the desert held the key to a deeper understanding.

Sarah's journey took her to the heart of the desert, where she was joined by a team of local archaeologists and Bedouin guides who were intimately familiar with the terrain. Together, they set out on an expedition to explore the hidden treasures buried beneath the sands of time.

The desert was both beautiful and unforgiving, its ever-changing landscape challenging even the most seasoned explorers. They traveled by 4x4 vehicles, the engines roaring as they raced over the dunes, leaving a trail of tire tracks that would soon be erased by the relentless wind. The sun blazed down, casting a shimmering haze over the horizon, and the temperature soared to a sweltering 110 degrees Fahrenheit.

As they ventured deeper into the desert, the guide, Ahmed, who hailed from a long line of desert dwellers, regaled Sarah with tales of the ancient trade routes that crisscrossed these arid lands. The desert, he explained, was not only a place of hardship but also a source of sustenance, where people had thrived for centuries. Sarah listened with rapt attention, realizing that the sands that now seemed barren and inhospitable were once teeming with life and commerce.

Their journey took them to the site of Al Zubarah, a once-thriving pearl fishing and trading port that had flourished in the 18th and 19th centuries. As they uncovered pottery fragments, anchor stones, and other artifacts, Sarah was reminded of how the riches of Qatar were not solely the result of oil and gas but had ancient roots in the lucrative pearl trade.

The team also ventured to the heart of the desert, where they discovered the remnants of a Bedouin settlement. It was a stark reminder of the nomadic lifestyle that had persisted for generations. The simple yet elegant design of the tents, the craftsmanship of the tools, and the resourcefulness of the people spoke volumes about the resilience of those who had called this harsh environment home.

But the desert held more than just remnants of human history. As the team continued their exploration, they stumbled upon an archaeological site that was truly extraordinary: the ruins of a desert palace that was believed to have been inhabited by a prominent local ruler during the 7th century. The intricate mosaics, ornate columns, and the faded grandeur of the palace painted a vivid picture of a bygone era when the desert was a place of opulence and culture.

As Sarah stood amidst the ruins, she couldn't help but marvel at the layers of history that the desert had preserved. It was a stark reminder that the wealth of Qatar was not merely a modern phenomenon but was deeply rooted in the passage of time and the legacy of those who had called this land home.

60. "DESERT MIRAGE: UNRAVELING THE WEALTH OF QATAR

With each discovery, Sarah felt a growing connection to the history of Qatar and its people. The desert, which had initially seemed like an enigma, was slowly unveiling its secrets, providing her with a profound appreciation for the depth of the nation's heritage.

As the expedition continued, Sarah knew that she was on the cusp of something extraordinary. The sands of time held the stories of generations, and she was determined to unearth the hidden riches that lay buried beneath the shifting dunes. The journey into Qatar's past had only just begun, and with each step, she was drawn deeper into the intriguing tapestry of history and wealth that defined this desert mirage.

3

Pearls of Heritage

As Dr. Sarah Reynolds delved deeper into her expedition to uncover the wealth and history of Qatar, she found herself drawn into the captivating world of pearls. Qatar's fortune was inextricably linked to these lustrous gems, which had shaped its history and culture for centuries.

The sun had barely begun its ascent when Sarah found herself standing on the shores of the Arabian Gulf, surrounded by a group of local pearl divers. Their faces were weathered by the harsh sun and saltwater, but their eyes sparkled with the wisdom of generations spent diving for treasure in the depths of the gulf.

The divers spoke in hushed tones about the pearls that had once made Qatar the "Pearl of the Gulf." For centuries, pearls had been the lifeblood of the Qatari economy, sustaining the nation's people and drawing traders from across the world. But it was more than just commerce; it was a way of life, a tradition that ran through the veins of the Qatari people.

Sarah was welcomed into the world of pearl diving, an art passed down through generations. She watched in awe as the divers prepared for their expedition, their traditional boats, or dhows, casting their shadow against the calm waters. Each diver carried a woven basket and a weighted belt, ready to descend into the gulf's emerald depths.

The process of pearl diving was not for the faint of heart. It required physical strength, stamina, and an intimate knowledge of the underwater world. As Sarah observed the divers plunge into the water, she couldn't help but feel a sense of reverence for their courage and the legacy they were upholding.

After hours of waiting, the divers resurfaced, their faces glistening with sweat and seawater. They carefully opened their baskets, revealing the iridescent pearls they had gathered. The pearls were exquisite, each a unique masterpiece of nature. As the divers held them up to the light, their colors danced in the morning sun, reflecting the rich history of Qatar.

Sarah was invited to join the divers on their return to shore, where a small village of pearl divers and their families had gathered. There, she witnessed the rituals and traditions that had persisted for centuries. Songs and stories were shared, and a feast was prepared, a celebration of the day's catch and a symbol of the resilience of a people who had weathered storms both at sea and on land.

It became clear to Sarah that the wealth of Qatar was not just the wealth of a nation; it was the wealth of a culture deeply rooted in the Gulf's waters and the pearls they produced. The pearl divers were the custodians of this heritage, passing down their knowledge and traditions to future generations.

As the sun began its descent, Sarah left the village with a newfound appreciation for the role that pearls had played in shaping Qatar's identity. The pearls of heritage were more than just gemstones; they were a symbol of resilience, culture, and the enduring spirit of a nation.

The journey to unravel the wealth of Qatar had taken an unexpected turn, revealing the intricate tapestry of history and culture that underpinned the desert mirage. Sarah couldn't help but wonder what other treasures lay hidden beneath the surface, waiting to be discovered as she continued her expedition into the heart of this enigmatic nation.

4

Echoes of the Past

Dr. Sarah Reynolds' quest to unravel the wealth and history of Qatar continued, each step leading her deeper into the heart of this desert mirage. Her journey had already uncovered the importance of pearls in Qatar's heritage, but there were more layers to be peeled back, more stories waiting to be unearthed.

One sunny morning, Sarah found herself standing at the threshold of Al Khor, a picturesque coastal town situated to the north of Doha. The gentle waves of the Arabian Gulf lapped against the shores, and the scent of the sea permeated the air. Al Khor was a place where time seemed to move at a different pace, preserving the traditions of Qatar's seafaring past.

As she explored the town, Sarah was struck by the juxtaposition of ancient and modern. Fishing boats, adorned with vibrant colors and intricate designs, were moored alongside modern fishing trawlers. The echoes of the past resonated in the intricate patterns that adorned the wooden dhows, a reminder of a time when the sea had been the lifeblood of the Qatari people.

Sarah's guide, Ahmed, introduced her to the Al Nuaimi family, renowned boat builders who had been crafting dhows for generations. The family's workshop was a treasure trove of craftsmanship, with half-finished dhows towering above her. The skills passed down through generations were still evident in the careful selection of wood and the precision of every cut.

The Al Nuaimi family shared stories of their ancestors, who had built dhows for pearl diving, trade, and fishing. They explained that these boats were not merely vessels; they were a testament to the craftsmanship and seafaring heritage of the Qatari people.

Sarah was then invited to join the family in the construction of a dhow. She was handed a chisel and shown how to shape the wood, her hands guided by skilled artisans. The process was meditative, a connection to the past and a tribute to the enduring spirit of craftsmanship.

As the dhow began to take shape, Sarah felt a sense of accomplishment and a deep appreciation for the traditions that were so deeply ingrained in Qatar's culture. The dhow symbolized not just the nation's seafaring past but also its ability to adapt and thrive in the modern world.

The next stop on her journey brought Sarah to the heart of Qatar's cultural heritage: the Souq Waqif. The bustling marketplace was a labyrinth of winding alleys and vibrant stalls, where merchants sold spices, textiles, handicrafts, and traditional Qatari garments. The souq was a celebration of tradition and a testament to the endurance of cultural practices.

As Sarah navigated the colorful maze, she discovered the Al Naimi family, who had been crafting traditional garments for generations. They were meticulous in their work, hand-stitching intricate designs on flowing abayas and ornate thobes. The garments they created were not just clothing; they were a reflection of Qatari identity and culture.

The family explained the significance of each design and the stories they conveyed. They spoke of the importance of preserving these traditions in a rapidly changing world. Sarah realized that, like the dhows, the garments were a link to the past, a thread connecting the modern Qatari identity with its rich history.

As the day came to a close, Sarah left the Souq Waqif with a deep sense of the resilience of Qatari culture. The echoes of the past were not distant; they were alive and well, woven into the fabric of everyday life.

Her journey was far from over, and with each discovery, she was drawn deeper into the complex tapestry of Qatar's wealth and history. The desert mirage was slowly giving way to a vibrant, multi-dimensional portrait of a nation that had navigated the sands of time with grace and determination.

5

The Modern Oasis

Dr. Sarah Reynolds' exploration of Qatar had taken her through the sands of time, uncovering the treasures of the nation's past, and the echoes of history still resonated in every corner she had visited. As she embarked on the next phase of her journey, she found herself in the heart of modern Qatar, where tradition and progress coexisted in harmony.

Doha, the capital city, was a testament to Qatar's rapid transformation. Skyscrapers kissed the sky, their reflective glass facades shimmering in the desert sun. The city's futuristic architecture stood in stark contrast to the ancient traditions Sarah had encountered in her previous explorations.

Sarah was welcomed by Hassan, a Qatari architect who was deeply passionate about the preservation of Qatar's heritage. Together, they embarked on a journey through the architectural marvels of the city, where tradition and modernity intersected in remarkable ways.

Their first stop was the Museum of Islamic Art, a pristine white structure designed by the renowned architect I. M. Pei. The museum showcased the beauty and diversity of Islamic art and culture, drawing visitors from around the world. Inside, Sarah marveled at the collection of ancient manuscripts, intricate calligraphy, and stunning ceramics, each piece a testament to the rich heritage of the Islamic world.

Hassan explained that the museum was a symbol of Qatar's commitment to preserving and celebrating its cultural roots while embracing a global perspective. It was a place where tradition and modernity converged, allowing the past to inform the present.

Their journey continued to Katara Cultural Village, a multifaceted complex designed to promote art, literature, and cultural exchange. The architecture of Katara was inspired by traditional Qatari design, with ornate arches and cooling wind towers, while the cultural offerings ranged from opera performances to exhibitions of local handicrafts. Sarah was struck by the dedication to preserving Qatari heritage and fostering a sense of cultural identity.

Amidst the opulent surroundings, Hassan shared stories of his own family's history, emphasizing the importance of family and tradition in Qatari culture. He explained how, even in the face of rapid change, Qataris held their traditions close to their hearts, cherishing the values and customs that had sustained them for generations.

Their final stop brought them to Msheireb Downtown Doha, a meticulously planned city district that aimed to blend sustainability and Qatari heritage. The district was a contemporary urban development, but every detail was rooted in the country's past. Traditional Qatari architecture, with its geometric patterns and open courtyards, was harmoniously integrated with state-of-the-art technology to create a sustainable and culturally rich environment.

As the sun began to set over Doha, Sarah couldn't help but be moved by the commitment of the people she had met to preserve their heritage while embracing the future. The wealth of Qatar was not just in its material prosperity but in the balance it struck between past and present, between tradition and modernity.

The journey had been a revelation, uncovering the layers of Qatar's history, from its pearling past to its modern-day accomplishments. Sarah's exploration had shown her that the desert mirage was, in fact, a dynamic and vibrant nation, where the spirit of resilience and cultural pride was as valuable as any treasure concealed beneath the shifting sands.

As she prepared to continue her expedition, Sarah knew that there were more layers to uncover, more stories to hear, and more to learn about the intricate wealth and history of Qatar. The chapters of her journey had taken her on an unforgettable odyssey, and there were more adventures to come in the rich tapestry of Qatar's story.

6

Beyond the Horizon

Dr. Sarah Reynolds' exploration of Qatar had led her through the pearls of heritage, echoes of the past, and the modern oasis that was Doha. As she ventured into the next phase of her journey, she found herself drawn further into the intricate web of Qatar's wealth and history, unearthing the layers that defined this enigmatic nation.

Her path took her to the desert once more, where she met with a group of Qatari conservationists and environmentalists. Qatar's commitment to preserving its natural resources was evident in their tireless efforts to protect the fragile desert ecosystem. With her newfound companions, Sarah embarked on a journey into the heart of Qatar's natural world.

The desert, a harsh and unforgiving environment, concealed a wealth of biodiversity. Sarah learned about the native flora and fauna that had adapted to life in the arid landscape, from the resilient desert plants to the elusive Arabian oryx, a symbol of the nation's conservation efforts.

Amidst the dunes, Sarah was introduced to a group of falconers, who shared their deep connection with the art of falconry. Falcons were not just birds of prey; they were a part of Qatar's cultural identity, and falconry had been practiced for generations. The bond between the falconers and their birds was profound, and their dedication to preserving this tradition was a testament to the enduring connection between Qatar's people and their environment.

The journey continued into the heart of the desert, where the team set up camp beneath a star-studded sky. The quietude of the desert at night was punctuated by stories around the campfire. The conservationists shared their hopes and dreams for a sustainable future, where the desert and its natural inhabitants would thrive alongside the nation's modern development.

The next morning, they visited the Al Reem Biosphere Reserve, where the group was welcomed by Dr. Ahmed Al-Malki, a Qatari scientist and conservationist. The reserve was a haven for biodiversity, with wetlands and lush vegetation thriving in the heart of the desert. Dr. Al-Malki explained the importance of these ecosystems and the efforts to protect them for future generations.

Sarah's experiences in the desert had revealed a different kind of wealth – the wealth of a nation's commitment to preserving its natural heritage and striking a harmonious balance between progress and conservation.

From the desert, Sarah's journey took her to Al Zubarah, the ancient pearl trading and fishing port she had visited earlier. This time, she explored the Al Zubarah Archaeological Site, a UNESCO World Heritage site that had been painstakingly excavated and preserved. The site told the story of Qatar's vibrant trade history, with its well-planned streets, grand houses, and marketplace.

Sarah was guided through the site by Dr. Mohammed Al Naimi, a Qatari archaeologist who had dedicated his life to uncovering the mysteries of Al Zubarah. As she walked through the ruins, she marveled at the evidence of a thriving community that had once called this place home. It was a testament to the trade and commerce that had shaped Qatar's history long before the discovery of oil.

As she left Al Zubarah, Sarah realized that Qatar's wealth was not just in its modern prosperity, its pearls, or its cultural heritage. It was in the dedication of its people to preserve the natural world, conserve its historical sites, and celebrate its traditions.

Sarah's expedition was far from over, and with each chapter of her journey, she was drawn deeper into the complex tapestry of Qatar's wealth and history. The desert mirage had transformed into a multi-faceted portrait of a nation that valued its past, embraced its present, and looked toward the horizon with hope and determination. There were more secrets to unveil, more stories to tell, and more treasures to discover in the intricate narrative of Qatar.

7

The Tapestry Unraveled

Dr. Sarah Reynolds' expedition to unravel the wealth and history of Qatar had been a captivating odyssey, taking her through pearls of heritage, echoes of the past, the modern oasis of Doha, the fragile desert ecosystem, and the commitment to conservation. Now, she stood on the cusp of the final chapter of her journey, ready to delve deeper into the intricate tapestry that defined Qatar.

Her next destination was a place that held a special significance in Qatar's history and culture: the Sheikh Faisal Bin Qassim Al Thani Museum. This magnificent institution was a living testament to the Qatari heritage, housing an unparalleled collection of artifacts, artworks, and historical relics. It was a treasure trove that spanned the spectrum of human history, from ancient manuscripts and archaeological finds to contemporary art.

Sheikh Faisal Al Thani, the visionary collector and philanthropist, personally welcomed Sarah to the museum. He shared the story of his passion for preserving Qatar's cultural legacy and the painstaking process of amassing such an extraordinary collection.

60. "DESERT MIRAGE: UNRAVELING THE WEALTH OF QATAR

As they meandered through the museum's vast galleries, Sheikh Faisal revealed the intricate connections between each piece. The artifacts told a story of human achievement and ingenuity, of the interplay between civilizations and cultures. Sarah was struck by the diversity and depth of the collection, which mirrored the diversity of Qatar itself.

One of the most remarkable pieces was an intricately carved wooden door from a Qatari fort, adorned with geometric patterns and Arabic calligraphy. The door was not just a work of art; it was a portal to the past, a symbol of Qatari craftsmanship, and a testament to the enduring spirit of the people who had built and lived within those fortifications.

The museum also housed a stunning display of traditional Qatari clothing, which showcased the artistry of Qatari tailors and the beauty of traditional textiles. Each garment was a living embodiment of the nation's cultural heritage, speaking to the rich history of its people and their deep connection to their roots.

Amidst the ancient relics and historical pieces, Sheikh Faisal revealed his vision for the museum. He aimed to create a space where the past could meet the present, where visitors could engage with Qatar's history and culture, and where the treasures of the past could inspire the aspirations of the future.

From the museum, Sarah's journey led her to Education City, an expansive hub for learning and innovation in Doha. The city was home to several prestigious universities, research centers, and institutions, each contributing to Qatar's vision of a knowledge-based society. The bustling campus was a testament to Qatar's investment in education and research, and its commitment to nurturing future leaders.

Sarah met with a group of students who shared their aspirations and dreams. Their passion for education, their thirst for knowledge, and their global perspectives painted a portrait of a new generation of Qataris who were ready to contribute to the nation's continued progress.

With her journey nearing its conclusion, Sarah realized that Qatar's wealth was not just material prosperity, cultural heritage, or a commitment to conservation. It was also in the commitment to education, research, and innovation that would shape the nation's future.

As Sarah prepared to bid farewell to Qatar, she reflected on the layers of history and culture she had uncovered. The wealth of Qatar was not just in its past or its present; it was in the enduring spirit of its people, their connection to their roots, and their determination to shape a brighter future.

The intricate tapestry of Qatar had been unraveled, revealing a story of resilience, cultural pride, and a vision for the future. The journey had been a revelation, and as Sarah left the desert mirage, she knew that the chapters she had uncovered would continue to inspire and captivate her for years to come.

8

The Ongoing Odyssey

Dr. Sarah Reynolds had concluded her initial expedition to Qatar, where she had unraveled the wealth and history of this captivating nation. But her journey was far from over. The desert mirage had beckoned her back to explore further, to delve deeper into the intricate tapestry that was Qatar.

Upon her return, Sarah's exploration began in the bustling heart of Doha, where she was welcomed by Dr. Ahmed Al-Sulaiti, a prominent Qatari historian and curator. Together, they embarked on a voyage through the National Museum of Qatar, a remarkable architectural marvel designed by Jean Nouvel. The museum was more than a repository of artifacts; it was a living story, a place where history came to life.

The museum's exhibits told the story of Qatar from its geological origins to its contemporary achievements. Sarah marveled at the immersive displays that showcased the nation's natural wonders, its bedouin heritage, its pearling legacy, and its meteoric rise as a global player in the energy market. She was reminded that the wealth of Qatar was not just a consequence of its vast natural resources but a result of the tenacity and vision of its people.

A highlight of the museum was the section dedicated to the political and economic transformation of the nation, showcasing how Qatar had navigated complex geopolitics to become a dynamic global player. The exhibits celebrated the diplomatic achievements, the investment in education, and the diverse cultural connections that had made Qatar an international crossroads.

In the museum's art wing, Sarah marveled at the work of contemporary Qatari artists who conveyed their perspectives on heritage and modernity through various mediums. The vibrant colors, bold strokes, and thought-provoking pieces showcased how artists were using their creativity to tell the story of a nation in transition.

Sarah's next destination was the Al Thakhira Mangroves, a unique ecosystem on the Qatari coast. Here, she met with a group of dedicated environmentalists who were passionate about preserving this fragile environment. Mangroves were a natural treasure, vital for coastal protection and nurturing marine life. The group's efforts to restore and protect these mangroves were a testament to Qatar's commitment to environmental sustainability.

As the sun dipped below the horizon, Sarah accompanied a group of astronomers to the Al Dosari Zoo and Game Reserve. Qatar's interest in astronomy was celebrated under the starlit desert sky, where they observed constellations, planets, and distant galaxies. The connection to the cosmos was a reminder that the wealth of Qatar extended beyond its terrestrial boundaries.

The journey continued to Education City, where Sarah had the opportunity to visit cutting-edge research centers and speak with scientists and innovators who were contributing to Qatar's knowledge-based economy. She was impressed by the depth of their commitment to research, technology, and the pursuit of groundbreaking solutions to global challenges.

At the end of her return journey, Sarah stood once again on the shores of the Arabian Gulf, watching the waves gently kiss the shoreline. She realized that the desert mirage had given way to a more profound understanding of Qatar's wealth. It was a wealth defined not only by material prosperity but by a rich history, vibrant culture, and a vision for a sustainable and innovative future.

The ongoing odyssey had become an indelible part of her life, a never-ending quest to explore the ever-evolving story of Qatar. As she prepared to depart once more, she knew that there were more chapters to be written, more discoveries to be made, and more adventures to be had in the intriguing narrative of Qatar's wealth and history.

9

Quest for Unity

Dr. Sarah Reynolds' ongoing odyssey to explore the wealth and history of Qatar had led her through layers of time, culture, and innovation. As she continued her journey, she found herself on a path that would unravel the essence of Qatar's unity, a theme deeply interwoven into the nation's narrative.

Sarah's next destination was the Al Wakra Museum, a gem nestled along the coast of the Arabian Gulf. Here, she was welcomed by Sheikh Rashid Al Thani, a passionate historian and curator. The museum was a testament to the unity of Qatar, preserving the heritage of Al Wakra, a coastal town with a rich history.

As Sheikh Rashid guided her through the museum's exhibits, Sarah marveled at the tapestry of Al Wakra's past. The town's fishing and pearling traditions were on vivid display, as were the customs and crafts that had shaped the lives of its people for generations. She saw the bonds of unity that held Al Wakra's community together, just as they did throughout Qatar.

Their journey continued to the heart of Qatar's desert, where Sarah met with a group of Bedouins who lived amidst the shifting sands. The Bedouins were the desert's nomadic custodians, preserving their cultural heritage and traditions passed down through generations. The unity of the Bedouin lifestyle, characterized by solidarity and resilience, was a stark contrast to the modern world's fast-paced living.

The desert, with its vast emptiness, reminded Sarah of the unity between Qatar's people and their ancestral land. As the sun set over the dunes, the Bedouins shared their stories around a campfire, further emphasizing the deep connection between the nation's past and present.

From the desert, Sarah journeyed to Al Khor, a place renowned for its fishing traditions. She was greeted by a group of fishermen who conveyed the importance of unity in their daily lives at sea. The challenges of the maritime profession required unwavering teamwork, trust, and unity to navigate the treacherous waters of the Arabian Gulf. Fishing was more than an occupation; it was a way of life that bound the community together.

The evening's feast was a communal effort, with fishermen and their families sharing the fruits of their labor. The unity around the dinner table mirrored the unity in their profession and their commitment to preserving the legacy of their forebears.

As her exploration continued, Sarah found herself in Souq Waqif once more. The bustling marketplace, with its intertwining alleyways, was a microcosm of Qatari culture. Merchants, shoppers, and artisans worked in harmony, representing the unity that was central to Qatar's identity.

Sarah met with a group of artisans who spoke passionately about their crafts, from weaving to pottery to calligraphy. These skills had been passed down through generations, a living testament to the unity of tradition and innovation.

The journey ended at the Unity Monument, a majestic sculpture in the heart of Doha. The monument was a symbol of Qatar's unity, standing as a reminder of the values and traditions that had held the nation together through the winds of change.

As she concluded her exploration, Sarah realized that the wealth of Qatar was not just in its material riches or historical treasures but in the unity of its people. Unity was the thread that wove through the tapestry of Qatar's history, culture, and future aspirations.

With each chapter of her ongoing odyssey, Sarah had uncovered a new layer of Qatar's multifaceted narrative. The desert mirage had become a living story, a story of unity that defined the nation and its people. As she left the shores of Qatar, she knew that her quest for unity was far from over, with more stories to discover, more experiences to share, and more adventures to come in the ever-evolving tale of Qatar's wealth and history.

10

A Future Unwritten

Dr. Sarah Reynolds' ongoing odyssey in Qatar had been an awe-inspiring journey, filled with revelations of wealth, history, unity, and the enduring spirit of a nation. As she embarked on the final leg of her expedition, she found herself drawn to a vision of Qatar's future, a chapter yet to be written.

Sarah's next destination was the Qatar Foundation, a visionary institution dedicated to nurturing the nation's knowledge-based society. Here, she met with Dr. Amina Al-Khater, a forward-thinking educator and the driving force behind Qatar Foundation's endeavors. They began their exploration in Education City, a vibrant hub for education and research.

Education City was a beacon of innovation, with leading universities, research centers, and startups shaping Qatar's future. The scientists, researchers, and students she encountered were at the forefront of groundbreaking discoveries and technological advancements, showcasing the nation's commitment to fostering a culture of learning and inquiry.

Their journey continued to Sidra Medicine, a state-of-the-art healthcare institution. Dr. Amina introduced Sarah to a team of doctors, nurses, and researchers dedicated to advancing medical knowledge and providing world-class healthcare. The collaboration between local and international experts reflected Qatar's vision for a healthy and prosperous future.

As Sarah explored the research labs, she realized that the wealth of Qatar extended beyond its resources to the potential of its people. Research and innovation were the building blocks of the nation's future, creating opportunities, solving challenges, and transforming the landscape of healthcare.

The expedition shifted to Hamad International Airport, a testament to Qatar's commitment to connectivity and global outreach. The airport's grandeur and state-of-the-art facilities showcased the nation's ambitions as a global player. It was a gateway not only to the world but to the future Qatar envisioned.

Sarah's journey took her to Al-Rayyan, a city renowned for its dedication to sports and a future that included the FIFA World Cup. She witnessed the construction of state-of-the-art stadiums, and she met with young athletes who embodied Qatar's commitment to nurturing talent and fostering unity through sports. The vision for the World Cup extended beyond a sporting event; it was a catalyst for change and development, a testament to Qatar's commitment to the future.

From Al-Rayyan, they traveled to Al-Shahaniya, where Sarah met with a group of scientists and environmentalists who were dedicated to preserving Qatar's natural heritage. The Al Dosari Zoo and Game Reserve had become a center for wildlife conservation, contributing to the future of Qatar's ecosystem.

Their journey culminated at the Qatar National Library, an architectural masterpiece that stood as a beacon of enlightenment. The library was a symbol of Qatar's dedication to knowledge, learning, and the preservation of culture. The books, manuscripts, and archives within its walls represented

60. "DESERT MIRAGE: UNRAVELING THE WEALTH OF QATAR

not only the past but the seeds of knowledge that would shape Qatar's future.

As she left the Qatar National Library, Sarah couldn't help but be filled with a sense of hope and anticipation. The wealth of Qatar was not just its natural resources or its history but its unwavering commitment to a future that was yet to be written.

With each chapter of her ongoing odyssey, Sarah had uncovered a new layer of Qatar's multifaceted narrative. The desert mirage had become a living story, a story of unity and a vision of the future. As she left the shores of Qatar, she knew that her quest to explore the wealth and history of this remarkable nation was an enduring one, with more stories to discover, more experiences to share, and more adventures to come in the ever-evolving tale of Qatar's wealth and history.

11

Building the Dream

Dr. Sarah Reynolds' journey through Qatar had been a profound odyssey, filled with discoveries of history, culture, unity, and a vision for the future. Her quest to explore the wealth and history of this remarkable nation had led her through a rich tapestry, and as she continued her expedition, she was drawn to the narrative of Qatar's visionary infrastructure projects.

Her next destination was the Lusail City development, a testament to Qatar's commitment to urban planning and sustainable growth. She was welcomed by Eng. Mohammed Al Naimi, an architect and urban planner, who guided her through the evolving landscape of this ambitious project.

Lusail City was more than just a modern urban development; it was a reflection of Qatar's vision for the future. The city was designed to be a sustainable and innovative metropolis, where residential areas, commercial districts, and green spaces harmoniously coexisted.

Eng. Al Naimi explained the importance of sustainable urban planning in Qatar's future. The city's architecture was not only aesthetic but also designed to withstand the challenges of the harsh desert climate, demonstrating the nation's dedication to environmental sustainability.

Their journey continued to the iconic Al Bayt Stadium, a spectacular venue designed for the upcoming FIFA World Cup. Sarah was deeply impressed by the scale and grandeur of the stadium, but what struck her most was its commitment to the future. The stadium's design incorporated traditional Qatari tents and showcased the nation's cultural heritage to the world.

As they ventured inside the stadium, Sarah met with the engineers and workers who were transforming the architect's dream into reality. Their dedication and pride in constructing a venue that would host the world's biggest sporting event demonstrated Qatar's commitment to embracing the future while honoring its traditions.

Sarah's expedition took her to the heart of Doha's West Bay, where she explored the Qatari Diar Tower, a skyscraper under construction. Eng. Nasser Al-Jaidah, a prominent architect and engineer, guided her through the towering structure, revealing the innovative design and advanced construction techniques.

The towering skyscrapers that adorned the skyline of Doha were more than just architectural marvels. They represented the ambition and determination of a nation striving for a prosperous future. These structures symbolized Qatar's commitment to progress and development on a global scale.

Their journey concluded at the National Museum of Qatar, where Sarah was joined by Dr. Hessa Al Jaber, a renowned museum curator and historian. The museum was a reflection of Qatar's wealth of cultural heritage and a testament to its commitment to preserving the past while embracing the future.

Inside, Dr. Hessa shared the significance of preserving and showcasing

Qatar's cultural heritage. The museum's exhibits were not just artifacts; they were a living connection to the past and an inspiration for future generations.

As Sarah left the National Museum of Qatar, she was filled with a sense of wonder and excitement for the future. The wealth of Qatar was not just its material prosperity or its history; it was its unwavering commitment to building a dream and shaping a better tomorrow.

With each chapter of her ongoing odyssey, Sarah had uncovered a new layer of Qatar's multifaceted narrative. The desert mirage had become a living story, a story of unity and a vision of the future. As she left the shores of Qatar, she knew that her quest to explore the wealth and history of this remarkable nation was an enduring one, with more stories to discover, more experiences to share, and more adventures to come in the ever-evolving tale of Qatar's wealth and history.

12

The Ever-Evolving Legacy

Dr. Sarah Reynolds' ongoing exploration of Qatar had been an enlightening odyssey, rich with discoveries of history, culture, unity, visionary infrastructure, and a dream for the future. Her quest to understand the wealth and history of this extraordinary nation had led her through a captivating narrative, and as she ventured deeper into her expedition, she was drawn to the concept of legacy and the ever-evolving nature of Qatar.

Her next destination was the Msheireb Museums, where she was welcomed by Dr. Ahmed Al-Malki, a Qatari historian and curator. The Msheireb Museums were a cluster of heritage institutions located in the heart of Msheireb Downtown Doha, dedicated to preserving and celebrating the nation's cultural legacy.

As they toured the museums, Dr. Al-Malki explained how each institution focused on a particular aspect of Qatari heritage. The Bin Jelmood House illuminated the history of the slave trade, a painful chapter in Qatar's past, while the Mohammed Bin Jassim House showcased the story of a noble Qatari family, and the Company House explored the development of early business enterprises.

The museums were not just historical landmarks but also a reflection of the evolving legacy of Qatar. They symbolized the nation's commitment to acknowledging its complex history, celebrating its cultural diversity, and shaping a future rooted in inclusivity and progress.

Their journey continued to the Barzan Towers, located in the northern region of Qatar. These historic watchtowers were perched atop a ridge and had long served as a guardian against potential threats. The Barzan Towers were a reminder of Qatar's unity and determination to safeguard its people, a legacy that continued to shape its national security efforts.

In Al Zubarah, Sarah revisited the UNESCO World Heritage site, now accompanied by Dr. Mohammed Al Naimi, the Qatari archaeologist. As they explored the excavated ruins, Dr. Al Naimi unveiled the ongoing work of preserving and unearthing the treasures of Al Zubarah. The commitment to heritage preservation was a testament to Qatar's ever-evolving legacy, where the past was cherished and cared for as a bridge to the future.

From Al Zubarah, they traveled to the Al Khor Wildlife Sanctuary, where Sarah met with a group of passionate environmentalists and ornithologists. The sanctuary was a thriving ecosystem for migratory birds and marine life, representing Qatar's dedication to protecting its natural heritage. The legacy of environmental conservation would be passed on to future generations, ensuring a sustainable and thriving ecosystem.

Their journey concluded at the Souq Waqif, where Sarah had experienced the living tapestry of Qatar's culture in her earlier chapters. This time, she joined a group of artisans who were teaching traditional crafts to young apprentices. The legacy of traditional crafts was being passed down through generations, ensuring that the cultural heritage of Qatar continued to thrive.

60. "DESERT MIRAGE: UNRAVELING THE WEALTH OF QATAR

As Sarah left the Souq Waqif, she was filled with a profound sense of the ever-evolving legacy of Qatar. The wealth of the nation was not just in its past or its present, but in the enduring spirit of its people, their connection to their roots, and their determination to shape a brighter future.

With each chapter of her ongoing odyssey, Sarah had uncovered a new layer of Qatar's multifaceted narrative. The desert mirage had transformed into a living story, a story of unity, a vision of the future, and a legacy that evolved with time. As she left the shores of Qatar, she knew that her quest to explore the wealth and history of this remarkable nation was an ongoing one, with more stories to discover, more experiences to share, and more adventures to come in the ever-evolving tale of Qatar's wealth and history.

13

Summary

Dr. Sarah Reynolds embarked on a captivating and ongoing expedition to explore the wealth and history of Qatar. Her journey spanned twelve chapters, each revealing a unique facet of the nation's multifaceted narrative.

Beginning with the "Desert Mirage," she uncovered the wealth of Qatar's natural resources and the importance of the pearl trade in its history. "Pearls of Heritage" delved into the rich tradition of pearl diving, highlighting the significance of these luminous gems.

In "Echoes of the Past," Sarah explored the seafaring heritage of Al Khor and the craftsmanship of the Al Nuaimi family, who built dhows. "The Modern Oasis" led her to the vibrant marketplace of Souq Waqif, where traditional crafts and the importance of cultural preservation were celebrated.

Chapter 5, "The Desert Ecosystem," explored Qatar's commitment to conservation, emphasizing the importance of the fragile desert ecosystem. In "Beyond the Horizon," Sarah delved into the archaeological treasures of Al Zubarah, shedding light on Qatar's trading history.

Chapter 7, "The Quest for Unity," celebrated the unity that defined Qatar's past and present. Sarah visited Al Wakra, connected with Bedouin nomads, and discovered the unity of fishermen in Al Khor.

"The Tapestry Unraveled" continued the journey at the Sheikh Faisal Bin Qassim Al Thani Museum, highlighting the unity of Qatar's people and their dedication to preserving cultural heritage. At Education City, Sarah witnessed the commitment to education, research, and innovation.

In "A Future Unwritten," Sarah explored Qatar's vision for the future, including urban planning, the FIFA World Cup, and sustainable architecture. "Building the Dream" revealed the determination to create a sustainable and innovative future, from Lusail City to Al Bayt Stadium.

In Chapter 12, "The Ever-Evolving Legacy," Sarah witnessed the ongoing commitment to preserving heritage, protecting the environment, and passing down traditional crafts to future generations.

Throughout her expedition, Sarah uncovered that Qatar's wealth was not just in its natural resources or its history, but in the unity, vision, and ever-evolving legacy of its people. As her journey continued, she knew there were more stories to discover, more experiences to share, and more adventures to come in the ever-evolving tale of Qatar's wealth and history.

www.ingramcontent.com/pod-product-compliance
Lightning Source LLC
LaVergne TN
LVHW010439070526
838199LV00066B/6087